# *Hell Bent For Election*

BOOKS BY
JAMES P. WARBURG

HELL BENT FOR ELECTION
IT'S UP TO US
THE MONEY MUDDLE

JAMES P. WARBURG

# Hell Bent For Election

DOUBLEDAY, DORAN & COMPANY, INC.
Garden City 1935 New York

PRINTED AT THE *Country Life Press*, GARDEN CITY, N. Y., U. S. A.

*To*
PHYLLIS
*Who helped compile the material*
*for this book*
*and made many helpful suggestions*
*while it was being written, and*

*To*
HALF-A-DOZEN FRIENDS
*who kindly read the manuscript*
*and gave much valuable help*
*and criticism.*

# PREFACE

As we approach the Presidential election of November, 1936, it is well for us to take stock of our present situation and to begin to make up our minds whether we want to continue along our present course—or change it.

Never in the history of our country has it been so necessary for every citizen to exercise intelligently the rights of citizenship.

Our country is faced with a crisis more serious than any mere "depression."

It is faced by a question more basic than unemployment or low prices or heavy debts.

When you and I go to the polls in November, 1936, we shall be voting, not for any one man, not for any one party, not for any one remedy or group of remedies, but for the continuance or discontinuance of the freedom we have enjoyed under what for want of a better name we call the American scheme of life.

I speak as one who had but little sympathy

with the Hoover administration; as one who in early 1933 had great hopes of what Franklin D. Roosevelt and his New Deal might bring to our distressed country, and as one who, after devoting no little time and sincere if ineffective effort towards the realization of these hopes, now feels not only disillusioned but convinced that the present administration is doing more harm than good, that Mr. Roosevelt is no more likely to change his basic characteristics than is a leopard to change his spots, and that the sooner we have done with him the better for the country.

I say this reluctantly because, in spite of what I think and shall say in subsequent pages, of Mr. Roosevelt, I have a feeling of affection for him which longs to deny what my reason tells me is undeniable. It is much as if I had a brother who was a locomotive engineer and developed color-blindness. I should continue to love my brother, but I should certainly not feel justified in urging his employers to continue entrusting him with the lives of others.

Why not then keep silent?

Certainly it would be more comfortable to do so. Certainly, for one who has a living to earn in this country, it would be more prudent, since, as I write this, the chances of Mr. Roosevelt's being reëlected are certainly no worse than even.

There is only one reason why I am impelled to write: it is the same reason that impels you to try to flag an express train before it reaches a broken culvert.

There is only one way to flag the train before it reaches the fatal spot, and that is to arouse the citizens of this country so that they will see the real issues of the coming campaign and to make them assert their will before it is too late. Toward this end I have been writing and speaking more or less continuously since late in 1933. And toward this end I shall continue until the tide is turned, so long as there is free speech in this country.

Until quite recently it was my feeling that the things to fight were wrong ideas and wrong policies rather than the men who originated them or put them into effect. Ideally speaking, I still think this to be true.

But we have got beyond the point of speaking ideally.

We have got beyond the point of separating the President, because he has a lovable personality, from his words and actions.

We have got beyond the point of blaming those who influence the President—be they radical or reactionary; be they in office or unofficial advisers.

In a speech at Butte, Mont., on September 19, 1932, Mr. Roosevelt himself said:

"Remember well that attitude and method—the way we do things, not just the way we say things—is nearly always the measure of one's sincerity."

We have come to the point where we must appraise Franklin D. Roosevelt by his own standard, for it is only upon a judgment so arrived at that we can intelligently decide whether to be for him or against him.

I am against him, and the purpose of this book is to tell you why.

There would be no reason to do this were it not for the very definite hope that my feelings may find an echo and my reasoning a response among those who share in the ever growing realization throughout the country that we are on the brink of a momentous decision.

JAMES P. WARBURG.

*August 31, 1935.*

# Introduction

## THE BASIS FOR APPRAISAL

IN SEEKING to reach an intelligent conclusion as to whether we want more of Mr. Roosevelt's leadership or whether we have had enough, it seems to me that there are several rather simple criteria—or, to use a Rooseveltian phrase, yardsticks—open to us:

1. How have his actions since he became President compared with his statements and promises, on the strength of which he was elected in November, 1932?

2. What are his purposes now, and do we agree with them?

3. How effective have been his actions taken to carry out his purposes, and how effective are his future actions likely to be?

4. Granted the importance, under our system of government, of the individuality of the chief executive, how do we feel after three years' experience about Mr. Roosevelt's individuality?

There may be other and more effective methods

of approach, but it seems to me these four yard-sticks offer us a pretty good opportunity to find out what we think.

One very important factor is of course omitted: namely, if not Mr. Roosevelt, then who? How, you may say, can I make up my mind about the elections of 1936 when I don't know who the other candidate is going to be—nor what he is going to stand for?

You can't, obviously. But it is just because of the absence of a definite alternative at the present time that I believe we are more likely to reach an objective conclusion about Mr. Roosevelt. Time enough later to make up our minds about the advantages and disadvantages of whatever alternative is offered.

And—more important—once you become convinced, if you do become convinced, as I have, that, barring an extreme radical or an extreme reactionary, almost anyone would be better than Mr. Roosevelt, who knows but what you may be able to take a hand in the shaping of the alternative?

Let us then proceed with our appraisal along the four lines of inquiry above suggested.

*Hell Bent For Election*

# 1

## WORDS VERSUS DEEDS

WHAT WAS THE BASIS upon which Franklin D. Roosevelt was entrusted by the American people with the difficult task of being their President? What caused the people to give him such an overwhelming victory at the polls in 1932?

I think we may answer this question by stating three major contributory factors:

1. The vote of November, 1932, was in large measure a vote against rather than a vote for. It was a vote not only against the unpopular Hoover government but in still greater measure a vote against all existing business and political leadership—in other words, a vote against those whom the people considered chiefly responsible for the depression. (To what extent they were responsible and to what extent the depression was caused by the World War and subsequent developments throughout the world need not concern us here. Certainly a wiser business and political leadership could have done much to avoid

some of the excessive manifestations of boom and collapse.)

2. The vote of November, 1932, was a vote for the avowed purposes and principles as expressed in the platform of the Democratic party and in the campaign speeches of Mr. Roosevelt. These documents were in effect a solemn covenant between the Democratic candidate and the people who voted for him.

Mr. Roosevelt said in effect, "If you make me your leader this is what I will do, or at least try to do. Mr. Hoover has told you what he will do, and Mr. Thomas has told you what he will do. It is up to you to choose whether to vote for Mr. Hoover, for Mr. Thomas, or for me." And on the basis of these statements of principle and policy, on the basis of these solemn promises, the American people went to the polls and overwhelmingly voted against Hoover, against Thomas, and elected Roosevelt.

3. Finally, there was the personality of the three candidates—or rather the personalities of Hoover and Roosevelt, for it can hardly be said that the personality of the Socialist candidate played any very important part. On the one hand there was Mr. Hoover, tired, frightened, with no hold over Congress and but little influence on the popular imagination; on the other hand we had

the fresh and dramatic figure of a man whose courage in conquering physical disability and whose innate sense of showmanship rendered him a popular hero made to order for the moment.

We are here concerned with the second of these contributory factors.

Let us have a look at some promises made in 1932.

## Unemployment and Labor Legislation

"1. A federal appropriation of $5,000,000,000 for immediate relief for those in need, to supplement state and local appropriations." (This promise seems to have been adequately fulfilled by the FERA.)

"2. A federal appropriation of $5,000,000,000 for public works and roads, reforestation, slum clearance, and decent homes for the workers, by federal government, states and cities." (This promise seems likewise to have been fulfilled by the PWA and CCC and other agencies.)

"3. Legislation providing for the acquisition of land, buildings and equipment necessary to put the unemployed to work producing food, fuel and clothing and for the erection of housing for their own use." (Something of this sort is being tried in various experimental communities in one of which Mrs. Roosevelt has taken a great interest likewise the Under Secretary of Agriculture, Rexford Tugwell, is working along these lines.)

"4. The six-hour day and the five-day week without a reduction of wages." (The Black bill for the establishment of a thirty-hour week was not passed by Congress.)

"5. A comprehensive and efficient system of free public employment agencies." (A comprehensive system has been established; its efficiency is a matter of opinion.)

"6. A compulsory system of unemployment compensation with adequate benefits, based on contributions by the government and by employers." (The Social Security Act provides for such a system, with additional contributions by employees.)

"7. Old age pensions for men and women sixty years of age and over." (Provided by Social Security Act for those over sixty-five years of age.)

"8. Health and maternity insurance." (Provided by Social Security program.)

"9. Improved systems of workmen's compensation and accident insurance." (See Senate bill 2793, introduced May 9, 1935, by Senator Wagner.)

"10. The abolition of child labor." (See NRA and proposed constitutional amendment.)

"11. Government aid to farmers and small home-owners to protect them against mortgage foreclosure, a moratorium on sales for nonpayment of taxes by destitute farmers and unemployed workers." (This promise was more than fulfilled, since a moratorium was extended not only for nonpayment of taxes but also for nonpayment of interest and principal of mortgage debts.)

"12. Adequate minimum wage laws." (These were established by the NRA.)

*Note:* The NRA and the Frazier Lemke Mortgage Moratorium Act were subsequently declared unconstitutional by the Supreme Court, but this does not alter the fact that Mr. Roosevelt tried to fulfill the promises involved in these two pieces of legislation.

So far, on the face of it, the above looks like a pretty complete record of fulfillment—in fact, an excellent record.

Why is it not, then, an excellent argument for Mr. Roosevelt's reëlection?

Because it is a record of fulfillment, not of promises made by Mr. Roosevelt or by the Democratic party, but a record of fulfillment of the promises made by the Socialist candidate, Mr. Norman Thomas.

The twelve points I have just enumerated are

word for word the first twelve planks in the platform of the Socialist party on which Mr. Thomas ran for President in 1932 and polled less than nine hundred thousand votes.

Does that surprise you?

And now let us see what the Democratic platform had to say on these subjects. Here are the planks on which Mr. Roosevelt polled almost twenty-three million votes:

"1. An immediate and drastic reduction of governmental expenditures by abolishing useless commissions and offices, consolidating departments and bureaus and eliminating extravagance, to accomplish a saving of not less than 25 per cent in the cost of federal government; and we call upon the Democratic party in the States to make a zealous effort to achieve a proportionate result." (As against this promise we have the whole galaxy of federal boards, commissions and offices which comprise the New Deal alphabet. We have added more than one hundred thousand federal employees, not counting those on relief or employed by the Public Works Administration or the Civilian Conservation Corps. As against the promise to reduce the cost of federal government by 25 per cent we have witnessed an increase such as there has never before been in the history of our country. That is how promise number one was fulfilled.)

"2. Maintenance of the national credit by a federal budget annually balanced on the basis of accurate executive estimates within revenues, raised by a system of taxation levied on the principle of ability to pay."

In regard to this plank Mr. Roosevelt had quite a little to say in his campaign speeches, particularly that delivered in Pittsburgh on October 29, 1932. The following excerpts are worth calling to mind.

a) "I regard reduction in federal spending as one of the most important issues in this campaign. In my opinion it is the most direct and effective contribution that government can make to business."

b) "Before any man enters my cabinet he must give me a twofold pledge of, first, absolute loyalty to the Democratic platform and especially the economy plank; and, second, complete coöperation with me looking to economy and reorganization of his department."

c) "Our federal extravagance and improvidence bear a double evil; our whole people and our business cannot carry its excessive burdens of taxation; second, our credit structure is impaired by

the unorthodox federal financing made necessary
by the unprecedented magnitude of these deficits.

"Instead of financing the billion-dollar deficit
of 1931 in the regular way, our government
simply absorbed that much of the lending capacity
of the banks, and, by so much, impaired the credit
available for business."

d) "I shall carry out the plain precept of our
party, which is to reduce the cost of the current
federal government operations by 25 per cent.
Of course that means a complete realignment of
the unprecedented bureaucracy that has assembled
in Washington in the last four years."

These are all quoted from Mr. Roosevelt's
own words spoken at Pittsburgh about three
weeks before he was elected.

Two other quotations will suffice to show that
Candidate Roosevelt's Pittsburgh speech—which
by now must have become somewhat of a bad
dream to President Roosevelt—was by no means
the only utterance of this sort made during the
campaign by the man who subsequently made
Mr. Hoover's expenditures seem like an attempt
at extravagance by a timid Scotchman.

On July 30, 1932, Candidate Roosevelt said:

"With these declarations the Democratic party
sets its face against the time-serving and dis-

astrous fiscal policy of recent years—when the depression began the administration, instead of reducing annual expenses to meet decreasing revenues, became sponsor for deficits, which at the end of this fiscal year will have added $5,000,-000,000 to the national debt. To meet this staggering deficit the administration has resorted to the type of inflation which has weakened public confidence in our credit both at home and abroad. . . . Let us have the courage to stop borrowing to meet deficits. Stop the deficits!"

And at Sioux City, Ia., on September 29, 1932, we have this little gem:

"I accuse the present administration of being the greatest spending administration in peace time in all our history, and which has piled bureau on bureau, commission on commission, and has failed to anticipate the dire needs of reduced earning power of our people."

And how were these promises fulfilled?

By the greatest series of budget deficits in the history of our country. The Hoover deficits, which Candidate Roosevelt found so indefensible, totaled about $7,000,000,000 in four years.

President Roosevelt's deficits in two years have totaled over $7,500,000,000.

President Roosevelt's expenditures, actual for

1934 and estimated for 1935 and 1936, amount to over $24,000,000,000.

According to the estimate of Chairman Buchanan of the House Appropriations Committee, the session of Congress which adjourned on August 26, 1935, appropriated some $10,250,-000,000.

From George Washington to Woodrow Wilson, which covers a period of 124 years, our federal government spent $24,521,845,000.

If Candidate Roosevelt's criticism of President Hoover's fiscal policy was sound—and the American people on November 4, 1932, seem to have indicated their feeling that it was sound—what must be said of President Roosevelt's fiscal policy?

## Relief, Public Works, and Social Security

In examining the Democratic platform of 1932 we find very little in regard to the above headings—at least, very little as compared to the Socialist platform or the subsequent actions of the Roosevelt administration.

Plank number five reads:

"Extension of federal credit *to the states* to provide unemployment relief wherever the diminishing resources of the states make it impossible for them to provide for the needy; expansion of the federal program of *necessary and useful* construction affected with a public interest, such as flood control and waterways, including the St. Lawrence Great Lakes deep waterways; the spread of employment by a substantial reduction in the hours of labor, the *encouragement* of the shorter week by applying that principle in government service; advance planning of public works."

And one other plank:

"We advocate unemployment and old-age insurance under state laws."

That is all you can find in the Democratic platform on the subject of relief expenditure, public works expenditure, and social security. That is all the majority of the American people voted for in 1932. They voted for a balanced budget, for reduced cost of federal government, for relief payments by the states and by the federal government to the states only where the states were unable to carry the burden alone. They voted for "advance planning of public works," for unemployment and old-age insurance under state laws.

Had they voted the Socialist ticket they would have voted for $5,000,000,000 of federal relief payments, for $5,000,000,000 of public works expenditure, for federal laws providing unemployment and old-age insurance, for federal control of wages and hours and working conditions—in short, for exactly what Mr. Roosevelt has given us, or tried to give us.

## Agriculture

As to farm relief, this is what the Democratic platform promised:

Plank number seven reads:

"For the restoration of agriculture, the nation's basic industry, we advocate better financing of farm mortgages through reorganized farm bank agencies at low rates of interest, on an amortization plan, giving preference to credits for the redemption of farms and homes sold under foreclosure; extension and development of the farm coöperative movement and effective control of crop surpluses so that our farmers may have the full benefit of the domestic market. Enactment of every constitutional measure that will aid the farmer to receive for basic farm commodities prices in excess of cost of production."

In another part of the Democratic platform under things condemned, we find:

"We condemn the extravagance of the Farm Board, its disastrous action which made the government a speculator in farm products, and the unsound policy of restricting agricultural production to the demands of domestic markets."

Could any more appropriate language be found in which to condemn the fundamental policies of the AAA? Is there anywhere in the Democratic platform any indication that Mr. Roosevelt intended to do the very things for which he condemned his predecessor, only on a vastly magnified scale, or that he intended to make his Secretary of Agriculture an absolute czar over the farmers of the United States? Did anyone who voted for Mr. Roosevelt on the strength of his preëlection promises think he was voting for paying bounties to farmers not to grow crops, to kill pigs, and to restrict production to the demands of the domestic market? Did anyone vote to place absolute power in the federal government to determine what farmers were to raise and how much and under what conditions?

Did anyone think Mr. Roosevelt, after condemning—justly I think—the actions of Mr. Hoover's Farm Board, would turn around and make Uncle Sam the world's biggest and stupidest speculator in agricultural products?

The platform promises relief on mortgages, and this was granted through the federal land banks and the Home Owners' Loan Corporation.

The platform says nothing about mortgage moratoria, although, as we have seen, the Socialist platform did.

The platform of the Democratic party says nothing about a central federal control over all agricultural enterprise with a view toward establishing a nationally planned economy directed from Washington.

But the Socialist platform contains this very clear statement:

"The creation of national, regional, and state land utilization boards for the purpose of discovering the best uses of the farming land of the country, in view of the joint needs of agriculture, industry, recreation, water supply, reforestation, etc., and to prepare the way for agricultural planning on a national, and ultimately on a world scale."

Again, in the light of subsequent action, it is hard to believe that these were the words of Norman Thomas's party and not the words of Franklin D. Roosevelt.

Here are three pertinent quotations of what Franklin D. Roosevelt did say:

1. On June 17, 1932: "We must at once take the Farm Board out of speculation in wheat and

cotton, try out a new plan to insure getting surplus crops out of the country without putting the government into business."

Making loans to cotton farmers against cotton at a price in excess of the world market price, and without the liability of the borrower to make good any loss, is not, I suppose, speculation!

And the "new plan" of getting surplus crops out of the country turns out to be a plan to destroy crops and prevent their being raised; to peg prices above the world price, thus stimulating foreign production and making reasonably sure that we shall never regain our lost foreign markets.

2. On July 2, 1932: "We should immediately repeal those provisions of law which compel the federal government to go into the market to purchase, to sell, or to speculate in farm products in a futile attempt to reduce farm surpluses."

Mr. Roosevelt might have added: "But we must pass a law permitting the government to do all these things."

3. On July 30, 1932: "Our party says clearly that not only must government income meet prospective expenditures, but this income must be obtained on the principle of ability to pay. This is

a declaration in favor of a graduated income inheritance and profits tax and against taxes on food and clothing."

And what is the processing tax, pray, except a tax on food and clothing, levied on all alike without the slightest reference to "ability to pay"?

*Note:* To avoid any misunderstanding of the above quotation in reference to income, inheritance, and profits taxes, it must be realized that Mr. Roosevelt at no time advocated or pledged an increase of such taxes. He merely reaffirmed his belief in the principle of such methods of taxation. In fact, in his Pittsburgh speech of October 19, 1932, he said: "I hope it will not be necessary to increase the present scale of taxes."

## Industry

And now as to industrial problems, the Democratic platform promised:

"Strict and impartial enforcement of the antitrust laws to prevent monopoly and unfair trade practices and the revision thereof for the better protection of labor and the small producer and distributor."

That is all you can find to foreshadow the whole gigantic NRA fiasco. That is all the people who voted for Mr. Roosevelt expected him to do.

Contrast this statement of policy with the first section of the Socialist platform, which I have already quoted, and which Mr. Roosevelt has so nearly fulfilled.

Instead of the promised "strict and impartial enforcement of the anti-trust laws," the NRA suspended the anti-trust laws, fostered monopoly, helped the big at the expense of the small industrialist, and produced some ten thousand printed pages of arbitrary rulings, which, until the Supreme Court made an end of this Roman holiday, had all the binding force of duly enacted laws.

Did anyone vote for business controlled by dictatorship?

Did anyone vote for arbitrary authority over wages, hours of work, prices, and conditions of competition to be placed in the hands of whatever individuals the President might choose to select?

Even the Socialist platform sought only to accomplish the reforms to which it was committed by the enactment of appropriate laws, or if necessary by an orderly amendment to the Constitution.

If we had had a Nazi or Fascist party in 1932, perhaps it might have written a platform that would conform to what Mr. Roosevelt tried to foist upon the country under the wings of the

Blue Eagle. But, if we had had a Nazi or Fascist party in 1932, I doubt if its candidate would have polled as many votes as Mr. Norman Thomas.

## The Currency

In taking up this highly controversial topic let me make it clear that I am not here concerned with the rightness or wrongness of what has been done, but only with its consistency or inconsistency with what the people voted for in 1932. To point out the inconsistency is not by any means to condemn as wrong. Some things that were done in the field of money and banking seemed to me right and justified; others seemed neither right nor justified.

What did we vote for as to currency in 1932?

Currency and fiscal policy go hand in hand. We have already seen that we voted for reduced governmental expenditures and for a balanced budget, and that Mr. Roosevelt condemned the policy of his predecessor in incurring budget deficits. Coupled with this statement as to fiscal policy the Democratic platform had this to say about the currency:

"A sound currency to be preserved at all hazards . . ."

That statement meant, if it meant anything to

the millions of people who voted for Roosevelt, a gold standard currency.

For one thing, you don't talk about "preserving" something that you haven't got. If Mr. Roosevelt had in mind making the basic changes in our currency which he afterwards made, it seems to me he would have said, "A sound currency to be established and thereafter preserved."

Apart, however, from any mere inference due to a choice of words, I think it is perfectly plain that no one thought he or she was voting for the reduction of the gold content of the dollar, nor for an irredeemable currency, nor for the repudiation of the gold clause in the bonds of the United States government, when voting for "a sound currency to be preserved at all hazards"—any more than anyone thought he or she was voting for a policy of piling up deficits when voting for Mr. Roosevelt.

The usual defense made by the New Dealers is that the course of events forced the action taken and that the resulting New Deal dollar is a "sound currency." I have stated fully in my previous writings why I do not think either statement correct, but that is not the point at issue here.

Suppose the "New Deal dollar" is a sound currency—which I do not think it is—certainly it is not what you or I or anyone else thought of when we went to the polls in the autumn of 1932. If Mr. Roosevelt had said in 1932 what he said in his famous message to the London Conference in July, 1933, do you think you would have voted for him? Suppose he had made this statement:

"Old fetishes of so-called international bankers" (such as the gold standard) "are being replaced by efforts to plan national currencies with the objective of giving to those currencies a continuing purchasing power which does not greatly vary in terms of the commodities and needs of modern civilization."

You yourself—if you are not familiar with such things—might not have been disturbed by such a statement. It might even have appealed to your emotional dislike of "so-called international bankers." But I can assure you that it would have deeply disturbed every responsible business executive, every large employer of labor, and the leaders of the labor organizations themselves. It would have disturbed them so profoundly that the repercussions of their disturbance would have been felt in every home in the country. At the very least it would have led to an instant demand that Mr. Roosevelt define what steps he intended to take in order to produce such a "planned national currency" which "would not vary greatly in terms of commodities and needs of modern civilization."

And if, as the result of such questions, the Democratic platform had stated as to currency:

1. We favor the establishment of a currency redeemable in gold only when as and if the Secretary of the Treasury shall consider it in the best interests of the nation to have it redeemable.

2. We favor confiscating all gold at its present price of $20.67 an ounce and thereafter raising the price to $35.

3. We favor a managed currency, managed by vesting in the executive at Washington complete and arbitrary authority to restore the price level of 1926 and thereafter maintain a dollar which will not vary in purchasing or debt-paying power, and

4. We favor the repudiation of the gold clause in the obligations of the United States government.

I do not hesitate to say that if the Democratic platform had contained these or similar planks, Mr. Roosevelt would never have been elected. (I have not even attempted to write a plank which would do justice to the Rooseveltian ideas on silver.)

And why should it not have contained such planks?

Why not, if, as the platform itself states, "a party platform is a covenant with the people to be faithfully kept by the party when entrusted with power, and that the people are entitled to know in plain words the terms of the contract to which they are asked to subscribe?"

Mr. Roosevelt did not make any very clear statements in amplification of the Democratic party's currency plank. I must say that I for one did not think any amplification was necessary. Others, however, who knew him better than I, did express distrust of the general endorsement of "a sound currency to be preserved at all hazards." As it turns out they were justified, but Mr. Roosevelt bitterly resented any such suspicion. Some of his statements in this regard are the following:

"It is obvious that sound money is an international necessity, not a domestic consideration for one nation alone."

Contrast this statement, made on July 30, 1932, with the message to the London Monetary Conference one year later, which I have already quoted.

On November 4, 1932, Mr. Roosevelt made this striking statement:

"One of the most commonly repeated misrepresentations by Republican speakers, including the

President, has been the claim that the Democratic position with regard to money has not been made sufficiently clear. The President is seeing visions of rubber dollars. This is only a part of his campaign of fear. I am not going to characterize these statements. I merely present the facts. The Democratic platform specifically declares: 'We advocate a sound currency to be preserved at all hazards.' That is plain English."

If that statement means anything at all, it certainly does not mean an intention to redefine completely what a "sound currency" is, and to go ahead and establish precisely the kind of "rubber dollar" that Mr. Hoover was afraid of.

And finally, how do you like this one?

"The business men of the country, battling hard to maintain their financial solvency and integrity, were told in blunt language in Des Moines, Iowa"—by President Hoover—"how close an escape the country had had some months ago from going off the gold standard. This, as has been clearly shown since, was a libel on the credit of the United States. . . .

"No adequate answer has been made to the magnificent philippic of Senator Glass the other night, in which he showed how unsound was this assertion. And I might add that Senator Glass made a devastating challenge that no responsible government would have sold to the country securities payable in gold if it knew that the promise, yes, the covenant embodied in these securities, was as dubious as the President of the United States claims it was."

On March 12, 1933—a week after Roosevelt had become President—the United States Treasury issued $800,000,000 of obligations payable "in United States gold coin of the present standard of value"—the same covenant above referred to by Mr. Roosevelt a few days before he was elected.

Additional securities followed shortly after, bearing the same covenant.

On May 7, 1933, President Roosevelt in a radio broadcast to the people announced his intention to repudiate this covenant.

And on June 5, 1933, the covenant was abrogated by act of Congress.

The point is not whether we agree or disagree with the President's judgment or reasoning. The point is that if he had such a conviction in regard to the gold clause and intended to act upon it, it would seem that the people had a right to know about it before they were asked to vote.

### Social Ownership

It would be an easy matter to continue quite a little further the comparison between the Democratic and Socialist platforms, but I think the point has already been made sufficiently clear. One might point out, for example, that recognition of Soviet Russia—which may have been a good or a bad thing—was a plank in the Socialist platform, but that neither Mr. Roosevelt nor the Democratic party let us in on the secret that it would be one of the first acts of the New Dealers when they came into power. Similarly, one may be for or against the elimination of tax-exempt securities; it was called for by the Socialist platform—not by the Democratic; Roosevelt is on record as favoring action towards this end.

To the reader who would like to pursue this matter further I recommend a careful reading of Dr. Tugwell's various writings, and a study of what avowed Socialists have to say about the New Deal.

I shall deal here with only one further item in the comparison. In a way it is the most important item of all.

Probably the reaction produced in the reader by what I have said so far is one of unpleasant surprise at the degree to which Mr. Roosevelt has fulfilled the promises of the Socialist platform. Most of us, I think, are only vaguely aware of what Socialism is or what Mr. Thomas promised in his platform. But the reader would at this point probably console himself with an observation something like this:

"After all, Socialism means public ownership of property as opposed to the private ownership to which we are accustomed under capitalism. What harm is there in it if Mr. Roosevelt adopted a few planks from the Socialist platform—what harm is there in it if he tries to improve the conditions of labor and agriculture—so long as the essential aim of Socialism, the public ownership of property, remains unrealized?"

To this very reasonable and probable reaction on the part of the reader I would like to make answer as follows:

1. Mr. Roosevelt's Secretary of the Treasury is publicly on record as favoring the ownership by the United States Treasury of the Federal Reserve banks.

2. The chairman of the Senate Committee on Interstate Commerce is publicly on record as favoring government ownership of the railroads.

3. The Tennessee Valley Authority exists and is operating. It is a huge power-producing and

distributing unit, set up in a region which was previously served by private industry. Mr. Norman Thomas commends it as an excellent example of pure Socialism.

The administration has publicized exceedingly well its "yardstick rates" in the Tennessee Valley. It has publicized less well the cost of the project. We have heard vaguely of an expenditure of $50,000,000, and when billions of dollars of the taxpayers' money are being tossed around, a mere $50,000,000 does not seem like very much.

But—it is not a mere $50,000,000 that is being spent in the Tennessee Valley. The plain truth of it is that the expenditures in the Tennessee Valley alone in the next five years will probably be something in excess of $300,000,000, and eventually something like a billion dollars.

That is on one item.

The administration's power projects form a network over the entire country. So far over $300,000,000 have been allotted on so-called "make ready appropriations." Much larger bills are to come.

The announced purpose is to bring light and power at less cost to the consumer.

The probable result will be the partial elimination of the private power companies, which means the partial wiping out of the savings of some five and a half million investors.

And, so far as cheaper light and power are concerned, Mr. Roosevelt said in a recent broadcast, "Facts are relentless."

So they are.

The fact here is:

If you deduct the subsidy of taxpayers' money from the Tennessee Valley Authority and from its rates now in effect, the "yardstick rates" of which the administration speaks so proudly are higher than the rates charged by the private companies serving the same territory; and, even with the advantages of the subsidies for which the taxpayer foots the bill, they are but slightly lower.

What has happened in the Tennessee Valley will doubtless happen in all the other government projects. It is difficult to see how it can be otherwise.

The taxpayer must always foot the bill for such examples of "pure Socialism."

In addition to pointing out these significant items I should like to draw the reader's attention to one other fact. We are living in a time when it is fashionable to be "social-minded." That in itself is a good thing. But we make the mistake of taking for granted that anything that is proposed for the good of the less fortunate elements in our social structure will actually redound to their benefit.

If Socialism really would be such a great thing for American labor, why is the American Federation of Labor opposed to it?

If Mr. Roosevelt is right in thinking that when we voted for him in 1932 we were really voting for what he has since given us, why did the Socialists poll only 884,781 votes?

Was it just because the American people liked Mr. Roosevelt so much better than Mr. Thomas?

Let me stress once more that this chapter is not intended as an argument against Socialism. I am against Socialism, and even more against its two misbegotten offspring, Communism and Fascism. But I am not arguing that case here. I am concerned solely with finding a fair answer to the first of our four questions:

"How have Mr. Roosevelt's actions since he became President compared with his statements and promises on the strength of which he was elected in November, 1932?"

I think a fair answer would be the following:

"He has done a few things that he promised to do—more things that he promised not to do—and still more things that his Socialist opponent promised to do."

In order to evaluate properly the true significance of this answer I think it is necessary to add:

"He has carried out his promises where it mattered least, and failed to do so where it mattered most."

He carried out, for example, the promises to repeal the eighteenth amendment (which would probably have been repealed under any administration); to give independence to the Philippines; to get us to adhere to the World Court (without success); and to put through the St. Lawrence Waterways Treaty (also without success).

He brought about a certain amount of hasty reform of our banking and investment system; the problem is by no means solved and requires careful study in order that the much needed real reform may some day be accomplished.

On the negative side he has failed to reduce the cost of federal government, to balance the budget, to maintain a "sound currency," to take government out of business, or to maintain the fundamental principles of the American order.

He has led us into an orgy of wild spending undreamed of prior to his administration, "piled commission on commission and bureau on bureau," and set up, or tried to set up, a federal dictatorship over all the various factors that affect the lives of our citizens.

He has flouted the Constitution which he swore an oath to support.

He has made a laughing stock of the sanctity of our national promises.

And he has done all this in the name of an emergency which, if it ever did justify such actions, certainly justifies them no longer.

# 2

## PRESENT PURPOSES

"It is not always fair," says Frank R. Kent, who is a good Democrat, "to quote a man's words against him after a long lapse of time. Often, on the spur of the moment, or in the heat of a fight, men say or write things for which they should not be held to too strict accountability. Conditions change and men change with them. No one should be condemned for changing his mind if he has a sound reason to change.

"Nevertheless," he continues, "men who hope to become President of the United States are expected to weigh their words well and mean what they say. Consistency and steadfastness in the White House are vital to the welfare of the nation. If the people cannot depend upon the promises of their President they are in a bad way. When a President or a candidate for the Presidency, in a prepared speech to the country, makes a solemn pledge and takes a definite and unequivocal stand, the obligation to live up to his words is far heavier than on the ordinary man."

We have seen in the preceding chapter that Franklin D. Roosevelt has failed badly to live up to this obligation.

We have seen very clearly that he did not keep his promises to the people.

But let us be fair. Conditions certainly did change rapidly and drastically during the winter of 1932–1933. Not enough, to be sure, to warrant or excuse so complete a reversal or so manifold a repudiation of solemn pledges as that perpetrated by Mr. Roosevelt, but enough, perhaps, to prevent our stopping right there and saying:

"Oh, well, a man who goes back on his promises like that doesn't belong in the White House under any circumstances."

And so we come to the second of the four yardsticks on the basis of which we were going to try to make up our minds about Mr. Roosevelt; namely:

"What are his present purposes and do we agree with them?"

Mr. Walter Lippmann once wrote of Mr. Roosevelt that "his mind is not very clear, his purposes are not simple, and his methods are not direct."

From my own first-hand observation during several months of close contact in the early days of the Roosevelt Administration, I honestly subscribe to this analysis. In fact, I should go a little further on all three counts.

I should say that Mr. Roosevelt's purposes consist of three major elements: the desire to be a hero; the desire to give everyone a "more abundant life"; and the desire to be "clever."

As to the first and last elements—the desire to be a hero and the desire to be clever—I shall have more to say when we come to consider Mr. Roosevelt's individuality—our fourth and last yardstick.

As to the second element, Mr. Roosevelt defined the "social objective" on June 7, 1935, as follows:

"To try to increase the security and happiness of a larger number of people in all occupations of life and in all parts of the country; to give them more of the good things of life; to give them a greater distribution, not only of wealth in the narrow terms, but of wealth in the wider terms; to give them places to go in the summertime—recreation; to give them assurance that they are not going to starve in their old age; to give honest business a chance to go ahead and make a reasonable profit, and to give everyone a chance to earn a living."

If this definition means anything it means that Mr. Roosevelt's objective is precisely the same as that of any other government. What government would not, if it could do these things, be glad to do them? What statesman, whether radical or reactionary, would not subscribe to this doctrine as a pious hope? How else could Mussolini, or Hitler, or Stalin, or the Emperor Haile Selassie of Abyssinia define his social objective?

But there is more than a mere naïve benevolence behind this general purpose. There is the conviction that Franklin Delano Roosevelt knows how to do these things, and that the way to do them is "to be clever" and not let the people in on what is really going on. There is the conviction that, given the widest possible range of "permissive powers"—the Rooseveltian synonym for dictatorial powers—Franklin Delano Roosevelt will be the Moses that leads his people out of the wilderness.

Behind this apparently vague and harmless statement of purpose there lurks the conviction that it is the proper function of the federal government at Washington to manage every detail of the economic life of the nation in such a way as to give everyone his or her proper share of "the good things of life."

Do you see where this leads?

It leads inevitably to the conclusion that "the good things of life" do not include freedom of speech and thought and action—do not, in fact, include any of the liberties which are so carefully guaranteed to us under the Constitution.

Mr. Roosevelt would indignantly deny this implication.

Mr. Roosevelt's enemies would indignantly affirm it and add that of course Mr. Roosevelt wants to be a dictator.

My own view is that Mr. Roosevelt's mind—which Mr. Lippmann says is "not very clear"—is so exceedingly unclear that he does not realize that the only way he can possibly do what he wants to do is by being a dictator. And that then he can only do it if, in addition to making himself omnipotent, he can also make himself omniscient.

Once upon a time Mr. Roosevelt realized that the centralization of power in the hands of the federal government would inevitably lead to disaster because it would break down upon the frailty of the human beings in whose hands the power would rest.

Once upon a time Mr. Roosevelt said:

"The doctrine of regulation and legislation by 'master minds,' in whose judgment and will all the people may gladly and quietly acquiesce, has been too glaringly apparent at Washington during these last ten years. Were it possible to find 'master minds' so unselfish, so willing to decide unhesitatingly against their own personal interests or private prejudices, men almost godlike in their ability to hold the scales of justice with an even hand, such a government might be to the interests of the country; but there are none such on our political horizon, and we cannot expect a complete reversal of all the teachings of history."

But that was said by Mr. Roosevelt on March 2, 1930, when, as Governor of New York, he was more interested in states' rights than he is today as President of the United States. That was said when Mr. Roosevelt still realized the limitations of human power.

Much as I dislike to say so, it is my honest conviction that Mr. Roosevelt has utterly lost his sense of proportion. He sees himself as the one man who can save the country, as the one man who can "save capitalism from itself," as the one man who knows what is good for us and what is not. He sees himself as indispensable. And when a man thinks of himself as being indispensable—

be it to his family, his business, his city, or his country—that man is headed for disaster.

But—to come back to our question—what are Mr. Roosevelt's present purposes, and do we agree with them?

I should say that his foremost purpose was the centralization of power in the federal government at Washington. We can see this purpose clearly expressed as to industry in the NRA, as to agriculture in the AAA, as to banking in the Eccles proposals, as to public utilities in the TVA and Wheeler-Rayburn bill, the Guffey bill, and others. We can see this purpose as to labor in the Wagner bill, as to "social security" in the FERA, the Social Security bill, and the Federal Housing Administration. We can see it in countless other expressions and manifestations every day.

Do we agree with this purpose?

No, we do not. And for reasons which no one has expressed better than Franklin D. Roosevelt at the time when he was Governor of the State of New York.

Here is some more of the speech from which I have just quoted:

"The preservation of this home rule by the states is not a cry of jealous commonwealths seeking their own aggrandizement at the expense of sister states. It is a fundamental necessity if we are to remain a truly united country. The whole success of our democracy has not been that it is a democracy wherein the will of a bare majority of the total inhabitants is imposed upon the minority, but because it has been a democracy where, through a dividing of government into units called states, the rights and interests of the minority have been respected and have always been given a voice in the control of our affairs. . . .

"Now, to bring about government by oligarchy masquerading as democracy, it is fundamentally essential that practically all authority and control be centralized in our national government. The individual sovereignty of our states must first be destroyed, except in mere minor matters of legislation. We are safe from the dangers of any such departure from the principles on which this country is founded just so long as the individual home rule of the states is scrupulously preserved and fought for whenever they seem in danger.

"Thus it will be seen that this home rule is a most important thing—the most vital thing—if we are to continue along the course on which we have so far progressed with such unprecedented success. . . .

"Let us remember that from the very beginning differences in climate, soil conditions, habits,
and mode of living in states separated by thousands of miles, rendered it necessary to give the
fullest individual latitude to the individual states.
Remembering that the mining states of the Rock-
ies, the fertile savannahs of the South, the prair-
ies of the West, and the rocky soil of the New
England states created many problems, introduced many factors in each locality which have
no existence in others, it is obvious that almost
every new or old problem of government must
be solved, if it is to be solved to the satisfaction
of the people of the whole country, by each state
in its own way."

That is my whole case against President Roosevelt's major purpose, far more ably stated by
Governor Roosevelt than I could hope to state
it myself.

In conclusion—so far as this second yardstick
is concerned—let me make it clear that there are
in the Roosevelt program many items with which,
as items, I am in thorough sympathy. I believe in
better working conditions; in the abolition of
child labor; in regulation to protect the public
interest in transportation and public utilities; in
social insurance; in bank reform, and so forth.

But I do not believe that these things are exclusively or even primarily the concern of federal government.

I do not believe in arbitrary authority to "regulate" being vested *in men* any more than is absolutely necessary.

I do believe in regulation *by duly enacted laws*.

I believe that the government's proper function is to act as a referee who sees that the rules are obeyed.

I do not believe the referee should from time to time pick up the ball and run with it himself.

Nor do I believe that the referee should from time to time change the rules of the game, unless a majority of all the players have first agreed to the proposed change.

I believe that Mr. Roosevelt fundamentally means well, that he honestly sees himself as upholding the American tradition, but that he has so hopelessly lost his bearings that he does not realize what road he is on nor where it leads.

For example, he did not realize when he stopped people in the South from planting cotton that they would inevitably use their land to plant something else. They happened to choose peanuts, and as a result Mr. Roosevelt soon found himself having to pay people not to plant peanuts. Even after this experience he did not realize that when he stopped the planting of peanuts he would be forced inevitably to the next step, which is perhaps the ultimate absurdity; namely, the control of the potato crop.

Most people do not as yet realize that we have on our books a new federal law under which it is to be made a penal offense for anyone to grow more than five bushels of potatoes without a special license; and not only that, but it is a penal offense punishable by a $1,000 fine or imprisonment for one year, or both, to buy any potatoes which are not either stamped with the special stamp or packed in the special kind of package prescribed by the law.

Mr. Roosevelt would have indignantly denied in 1933 that his AAA program would lead to such a law governing the purchase and sale of potatoes; just as he would doubtless deny with equal indignation today that the laws already enacted will inevitably lead to more and more federal regulation unless and until the whole program of centralized control is abandoned.

I believe that Mr. Roosevelt is so charmed with the fun of brandishing the band leader's baton at the head of the parade, so pleased with the picture he sees of himself, that he is no longer capable of recognizing that the human power to lead is limited, that the "new ideas" of leadership dished up to him by his bright young men in the Brain Trust are nothing but old ideas that have been tried before, and that one cannot uphold the social order defined in the Constitution and at the same time undermine it.

Could any President, who had not lost his sense of proportion, have written, as Franklin D. Roosevelt wrote on July 6, 1935, to the chairman of a legislative committee of Congress, urging the passage of a piece of legislation (the Guffey-Snyder coal bill) :

"I hope your committee will not permit any doubt as to the constitutionality, however reasonable, to block the suggested legislation."

Could any President who had not lost his sense of proportion, have characterized a unanimous decision of the United States Supreme Court (the NRA decision) as putting the country back "to the horse and buggy days"?

"I, Franklin Delano Roosevelt, do solemnly swear that I will faithfully execute the office of the President of the United States and will, to the best of my ability, preserve, protect, and defend the Constitution of the United States, so help me God."

Could any man, who swore that oath on March 4, 1933, and who had not lost his sense of proportion, express in no uncertain terms his desire that Congress disregard any doubts, "however reasonable," as to the constitutionality of a measure the passage of which he himself was demanding?

So much for the second yardstick.

# 3

## ARE MR. ROOSEVELT'S ACTIONS EFFECTIVE?

IN THE PRECEDING CHAPTER I have stated what I conceive to be Mr. Roosevelt's major purpose —that is, the centralization of power in the federal government, to the end that the federal government may be able to give the people "a more abundant life." I have stated that I do not believe in this purpose, because, as Mr. Roosevelt himself pointed out a few years ago, centralization of power in the federal government is not, in this country, the way to arrive at "a more abundant life"—unless we wish to change all our basic concepts as to what constitutes freedom and happiness.

(I might have added that, when Mr. Roosevelt seeks to centralize power in the federal government, he seeks in effect to centralize it, not in the federal government as a whole, but in the Executive—that is, in himself. I might have added that, if there is to be centralized power, it would be better and safer to centralize it in a carefully balanced government in which the legislative and judiciary branches are equally important with the executive.)

It is not necessary to go further into detail. Most citizens are not particularly interested in the Constitution as a theory. They are interested in the practical advantages and disadvantages of living in a country governed as ours has been governed under the Constitution, or of living in a country where supreme authority is vested in a central government.

What I am saying is that you cannot have both.

What I am saying is that Mr. Roosevelt believes in centralized authority—although formerly he did not—and that I think he is wrong in now holding that adherence to our traditional order is going back to "the horse and buggy days."

And so, having answered our first two questions, we come to the third:

"How effective have been Mr. Roosevelt's actions taken to accomplish his purposes, and how effective are his future actions likely to be?"

I should answer this rather difficult question as follows:

1. His actions taken to accomplish the centralization of power in a federal bureaucracy have been highly effective. He has accomplished a

centralization of power such as we have never seen in this country, such as was never contemplated or permitted by the Constitution, and such as undoubtedly will be found in large measure unconstitutional by the Supreme Court.

2. His actions taken, by means of the vast centralized powers obtained from a driven and bewildered Congress, in the direction of producing "a more abundant life" have been very largely ineffective.

3. Where these latter actions have been effective—as in the case of relief payments—their effectiveness is very often of an obviously temporary nature. Four and a half billion dollars a year will effectively prevent millions of people from starving, but only so long as you go on spending the money to feed them.

To take another example, the agricultural relief program has been effective in the sense that it has put money in the hands of the farmers, but it has not solved their problem. If the AAA is declared unconstitutional—as it seems likely it will be—a new method will have to be devised. And even if this does not happen, the "effectiveness" of the AAA is limited by the length of time that its costs can be supported.

But that is not the worst of it.

When you say a thing is effective you really mean two things:

You mean that it works—that is, does what it is supposed to do, and

You mean that it gives you what is wanted without incurring a disproportionate sacrifice.

It is my considered opinion that most of Mr. Roosevelt's actions which can be considered effective in the first sense are flagrantly ineffective in the second.

Take again the same two examples of relief payments and the AAA.

As to relief—which is undoubtedly the most difficult problem—Mr. Roosevelt was faced with two undeniable facts:

1. Some form of relief payments had to be devised to keep the unemployed from starving.

2. Whatever money was to be spent for this purpose had to come from the people, eventually, in the form of taxes.

This was a problem that existed for months before Mr. Roosevelt took office—a problem that he had ample time to think about before he became President, or even President-elect.

Knowing the problem and having thought about it, he took in 1932 a very definite, and to my mind correct, position:

He condemned budget deficits.

He recognized that no government can spend more than it can raise by taxation without rendering ineffective whatever other actions it may take.

He recognized that "taxes are paid in the sweat of every man who labors." (Pittsburgh, October 19, 1932.)

He recognized that relief was primarily a concern of the states, and that the federal government should confine itself to aiding the states whenever "the diminishing resources of the states made it impossible for them to carry the burden alone."

The implication of such a program—which was, I think, the right program—was that unemployment could be cured only by a revival of business activity; that the most the federal government could do, pending such a revival, was to help the states carry out whatever relief programs the citizens of each of the states might determine; and that it was certainly not the function of the federal government to guarantee every employable a job.

That is what Candidate Roosevelt said he believed.

That is not what President Roosevelt says he believes now.

President Roosevelt has forgotten what happens to the people of a country whose government consistently spends more than its income.

President Roosevelt has forgotten that the money he is handing out so generously is money which will have to be paid "in the sweat of every man who labors."

President Roosevelt has come to believe in the omnipotence and omniscience of a central government bureaucracy which will determine for the whole country what it shall eat and drink and do with its leisure time, and which will find jobs for everyone that will assure them of "a more abundant life."

I am told that this is "good politics."

I fervently hope that 1936 will show that it is not.

I fervently hope and believe that the American people will realize:

1. That some day they will have to pay in their own sweat for Mr. Roosevelt's generosity —as well as for his extravagance in setting up a huge bureaucracy.

2. That a different relief program, such as that advocated by Mr. Roosevelt in 1932, would have produced the same amount of relief without retarding recovery and without abandoning the fundamental principles of home rule.

3. That there is at least some danger—to put

it mildly—in the fact that Mr. Roosevelt has put himself in a position where, in addition to the usual "patronage," he can swing a four and one half billion dollar relief fund over the heads of Congressmen, whenever they show any signs of becoming restive under the apparently endless sequence of "must" legislation demanded by the White House.

And now as to the other example, the Roosevelt agricultural program:

The idea behind the AAA when it was established was supposed to be the restoration of the purchasing power of the farmer. Ultimately this was to have been accomplished by "adjustment" of production to consumption through crop control. In the meantime this ultimate objective was to be hastened by paying bounties to agricultural producers, provided they would agree to reduce their production in accordance with plans made at Washington. These bounties were to be financed by "processing taxes" levied upon the consumers of farm products.

The processing taxes are probably unconstitutional and are certainly the kind of tax on food and clothing against which Mr. Roosevelt specifically committed himself. But that is not the main point.

The main point emerges clearly as we watch the development of the administration of this program of "adjustment." Originally the act was written to operate only through the voluntary coöperation of the farmer. As time went on we had less and less coöperation and more and more coercion. As time went on we had the Bankhead Act, which contains no semblance of voluntary coöperation by the farmer, and, as I write this, we have just witnessed the passage by Congress of certain administration-sponsored amendments to the AAA which remove once and for all any doubt as to where this program is leading.

The administration refers to these amendments as mere "clarifying amendments." As a matter of fact, they are much more than that. But I do not object to calling them "clarifying amendments" because they do clarify, beyond any question of doubt, what Mr. Roosevelt is trying to do. Fortunately we have once more President Roosevelt's own words upon which to base our judgment.

When he was making his now famous "horse-and-buggy" complaint upon the invalidation of the NRA by the Supreme Court, President Roosevelt took particular pains to point out the probable effect of this decision upon the rest of the New Deal. He said that the same reasoning which had caused the Court unanimously to hold the NRA unconstitutional would probably likewise cause it to invalidate the whole AAA, and he added with obvious chagrin that this would mean a return to "the old policy that every farmer was a lord on his own farm, free to raise whatever and as much of any crop as he pleased."

It is quite possible that I am completely wrong in my interpretation of what the American people and particularly the American farmer want. I am no politician, and Mr. Roosevelt is said to be "the best politician we have ever had in the White House." But it seems to me that to have every farmer "a lord on his own farm, free to raise whatever and as much of any crop as he pleases," is not such a terrible thing at all. In fact, it seems to me a pretty good thing—certainly a far better thing than having Messrs. Wallace and Tugwell sitting in Washington and figuring out what and how much every farmer is to raise—certainly a far better thing than having a law which forbids us to raise more than five bushels of potatoes and which tries to make us into a nation of spies and informers.

We are a free people and not a race of Russian peasants; and, with all due respect to Mr. Roosevelt and his bureaucratic experts, I see no reason to suppose that they are the "men almost godlike in their ability to hold the scales of justice with an even hand" whose existence Mr. Roosevelt himself so wisely doubted back in March, 1930.

So, then, I should say that the AAA—our second example—was effective (though not as effective as the drought) in temporarily raising the farmer's purchasing power, without, however, leaving the farmer one bit better off than he was before, when and if the AAA is invalidated by the Supreme Court.

And I should say that this temporary relief for the farmer was acquired at the expense of all our citizens, without reference to "ability to pay," and at the cost to our farmers of their American birthright of freedom.

So much for the Roosevelt policies that might be called temporarily effective but whose temporary effectiveness has been purchased at what to me at least would seem too great a cost. In this category I should place most of the so-called recovery measures—the spending program, the NRA, the AAA, and all the countless federal agencies by which Mr. Roosevelt has sought to impose a planned economy upon this nation.

The New Dealers would answer this statement by raising a cry of "Laissez-faire." Anyone who says what I have said—or in fact anyone who disagrees with them—is instantly accused of three things: ignorance, self-interest, and a desire to do nothing.

The charge of ignorance or self-interest does not trouble me. We are all ignorant, and we are all to a certain extent self-interested. The only difference is that some of us do not realize it.

As to the charge of laissez-faire my answer is this:

A do-nothing policy would be less harmful than a policy of muddle-headed meddling, but I do not advocate a do-nothing policy. I advocate a policy for the federal government of doing what it is intended to do under the Constitution, and of leaving to the states and smaller units of society down to and including the individual, the functions that properly belong to them—including the function of making their own mistakes.

I advocate—if I can understand plain English —exactly what Mr. Roosevelt advocated before he moved from the Executive Mansion at Albany to the White House.

And now let me give you one example of another kind of Roosevelt thinking, for which it cannot even be said that it is *temporarily* effective.

On June 19, 1935, Mr. Roosevelt sent a surprise message to Congress demanding that a new program of taxation be enacted. In this message he endorsed the principle that taxes should not only be levied to produce revenue but that they should carry out the social objective of preventing the accumulation of great wealth in the hands of the few. "Our present revenue laws," he said, "have done little to prevent an unjust concentration of wealth and economic power."

Whether we agree with this principle is not the point at issue here (for my own part I agree that excessive concentration of wealth and power is an evil, but I am inclined to think that the cure is to be sought in the enlightenment of self-interest by a gradual process of education rather than in an attempt to legislate a higher morality and a greater social consciousness. Nevertheless, there are some things that can be done—such as the elimination of tax-exempt securities—which I have advocated elsewhere).

We are concerned here with the effectiveness of the actions suggested by Mr. Roosevelt to accomplish the stated objective.

His three major recommendations were:

1. Heavy inheritance taxes on "very large amounts."

2. An increase in the income taxes on "very great individual incomes."

3. A graduated income tax on corporations.

I am not concerned here with the fact that this

whole proposal was so vague and nebulous as to arouse doubt as to its sincerity. The thing that I find interesting is the third proposal.

The President recommended "the substitution of a corporation income tax graduated according to the size of corporation income in place of the present uniform corporation income tax of 13¾ per cent. The rate for smaller corporations might well be reduced to 10¾ per cent, and the rates graduated upwards to a rate of 16¾ per cent on net income in the case of the largest corporations. . . ."

Do you see what this means?

It means that a corporation such as the American Tel. & Tel. Company would pay a tax of 16¾ per cent of its income, merely because it is one of the largest corporations, whereas the X Company, which is small, would pay only 10¾ per cent.

But the American Tel. & Tel. Company is owned by some 675,000* stockholders, with average holdings of 28 shares, whereas the X Company may be owned entirely by a rich man and his immediate family.

The result of the President's proposal would

*Of these 675,000 stockholders, 379,000 are women, and more than 100,000 are Bell System employees, according to the company's 1934 Annual Report.

be that a tax of 16¾ per cent would have to be taken out of the earnings available for the dividends to be paid to 675,000 small shareholders of a large corporation, while only 10¾ per cent would be deducted from the earnings available for dividends to the few large shareholders in the small corporation.

Was there ever a better example of putting the cart before the horse?

The President's avowed purpose is to prevent the rich man from getting too rich and to help the poor man get richer.

So what does he do?

He recommends a measure which, if enacted, might tax the hundreds of thousands of small investors one sixth of their possible dividends while taxing the few large owners of small corporations only one tenth of their possible dividends.

The obvious absurdity of this proposal was recognized by Congress which, under the pressure of the Democratic majority, enacted a face-saving graduated corporation tax so as to avoid completely repudiating the President.

Similarly the President is said to have insisted that charitable contributions by corporations should no longer be tax-exempt, a proposal which would have had the obvious effect of withdrawing the major support from the nation's charitable institutions at a time when it was needed as never before. This proposal, fortunately, was not adopted by Congress.

Nor are these the only fallacies involved in this latest vagary of the Roosevelt mind, but they suffice to illustrate the point I am making here.

Another example of the same sort of unclear thinking was the much ballyhooed work relief program, which was sprung upon the country in January, 1935. The President asked for an appropriation of $4,800,000,000 and announced that with this sum he would create useful jobs for 3,500,000 unemployed.

It does not take much of a mathematician to figure out the ridiculousness of such a proposal. Divide your men into your dollars and you have something under $1,400 per man. Is it possible that that is what the President did? Is it possible that he did not realize that in even the most economical work relief program of useful work the cost of materials, transportation, and overhead will take a very large part of the available funds? That the President did not have in mind the leaf-raking sort of jobs which he tried in the CWA experiment was amply clear from his message of January 4. What he had in mind were the sort of jobs that require expensive planning, skilled labor, expensive machinery and tools, and plenty of building materials.

The proof of the pudding is in the eating of it. There has been no miracle.

The President has found no bright young man capable of creating the sort of useful jobs that can be done by the unemployed without incurring tremendous costs other than wages for unskilled labor, and so, after all the blaring of trumpets, we are back again to the old CWA expedient of makeshift jobs.

"But," you may say, "don't you agree with the President that work relief is much better for the morale of the unemployed than a dole or makeshift jobs?"

Of course I do. Much better—if it can be done without bankrupting the nation or establishing a central bureaucratic dictatorship. But my plain ordinary common sense tells me that it cannot be done by any of the methods that have been, or are likely to be, devised by Mr. Roosevelt's bright young men, no matter how many rabbits their combined hats may contain.

It is interesting to note that in this type of ineffectiveness Mr. Roosevelt suffers not only from the malady of excessive planning—as in the NRA and AAA examples—but from a combination of too much "planning" in the basic concept of the scheme and too little planning in its execution.

In the early days of the administration I was shocked by the slapdash slipshod methods by which the administration sought to solve problems that had baffled the wisest minds for years. I was shocked then by Mr. Roosevelt's blithe and carefree manner of dealing with matters which affected the lives of not only 125,000,000 Americans, but also the lives of countless millions throughout the world. In those days I used to console myself by saying, "After all, this is an emergency. What do you expect the man to do? He cannot suddenly become a profound student of economics, and he must meet the situation that confronts him."

I even used to try to make myself believe, as most of the others around the President believed, that he had some sort of mysterious sixth sense—some sort of instinctive inspiration—which made knowledge of facts and careful study of ideas unnecessary.

But as time went on I came to realize more and more that Mr. Roosevelt's offhand methods had nothing whatsoever to do with the emergency; and that his alleged sixth sense was mostly a rather pronounced flair for the dramatic.

It is not pleasant to come to the conclusion

that there is no excuse for the heedless haste and casual disregard of realities which have characterized so many of Mr. Roosevelt's actions. And yet that is the conclusion to which I must come in answering our third question.

And so my answer is this:

Mr. Roosevelt's actions have on the whole been ineffective and are likely to continue to be ineffective so long as he remains in the White House.

He seeks to do too much—more than any man in any position could realistically hope to do—and certainly more than we can permit any man in the White House to do if we want to preserve the American scheme of life.

And in addition to attempting too much he does what he attempts to do too thoughtlessly, too hastily, and without first acquiring sufficient knowledge.

And further, it is my considered opinion for what it may be worth that, as time goes on and as the popular applause upon which Mr. Roosevelt is so dependent becomes less and less audible, he will become more and more feverish in his activity, more and more grandiose in his schemes, and less and less effective in putting them into action.

# 4

## PRESIDENT ROOSEVELT'S INDIVIDUALITY

WE COME NOW to the last of our four yardsticks:
"Granted the importance under the American
system of government of the individuality of the
chief executive, what do we think, in the light of
our experience so far, of Mr. Roosevelt's individuality?"

This is by far the most difficult of the four
questions, because we find ourselves here almost
entirely in the realm of opinion. The first question was easy to answer, because Mr. Roosevelt's
preëlection promises and post-election actions are
a matter of public record. The second question,
while requiring a certain amount of analysis of
Mr. Roosevelt's purposes, was also relatively
easy, because all we had to do was to let Mr.
Roosevelt's deeds define his purpose and his
words condemn it. The third question, which we
have just answered, involved opinion to a certain

extent, but I think the reader will agree that the facts alone present a pretty clear answer.

But, in discussing the individuality of a man—which is by rights the job of a trained psychologist —one is compelled to reach conclusions which are influenced by one's own interpretation of what evidence is available.

I shall therefore confine myself in this chapter to the bare statement of the only hypothesis which seems to me to fit the facts.

I have heard many people question Mr. Roosevelt's sincerity, and I have heard many people question his intelligence.

The hypothesis which I wish to state is that Mr. Roosevelt is neither insincere nor unintelligent, but that his mind, and consequently his words and actions, are dominated by his emotional desires, likes, and dislikes to an unusual extent, and that this domination of the mind by the emotions is what causes his inconsistencies and accounts for all the extraordinary contradictions which we have noted in preceding chapters.

I believe that Mr. Roosevelt's primary desire is a desire to be agreeable, that is, to be liked and admired by whomsoever he happens to be with at the moment.

I believe that Mr. Roosevelt wanted to become President and wants to remain President primarily because being President expresses, more than anything else could express it, the fact of being liked and admired by the greatest possible number of people.

If one accepts this hypothesis, it explains both the words and actions which have caused his sincerity and intelligence to be questioned; it explains the extraordinary instability of Mr. Roosevelt's basic ideas as illustrated by his preëlection promises and his post-election actions; it explains how he can agree with one man that the wind is from the east and with another that it is from the west; it explains how he can adopt the Socialist platform and deny its label.

You may say that the distinction I am drawing is a fine one; and so it is; but it is nevertheless to my mind an important distinction.

When a man agrees that the wind is from the east, knowing it is from the west, I would call such a man insincere, but when a man agrees that the wind is from the east because at the moment he is honestly convinced that it is from the east, I would not call him insincere, even though I might recognize that his apparent conviction was not an intellectual conviction but an emotional domination of his mind arising from the desire to agree with another man.

I am not saying that this is an admirable characteristic. I am merely saying that it is different from what I would call insincerity.

Similarly, if one accepts this hypothesis, it explains the stupidity and superficiality of which Mr. Roosevelt is frequently accused.

From my own observation, I should say that Mr. Roosevelt's mind is quick, his memory excellent, and that he has an extraordinary capacity to grasp new material.

On the other hand, this excellent intellectual machinery has often seemed to me to be impeded by very strong emotional interference—by the interference, in other words, of conscious and subconscious desires, likes and dislikes.

Mr. Roosevelt's mind is quick to the point of nimbleness when he is interested or pleased. It is slow to the point of being stationary when he is not.

When he is pleased he is animated, and those who have caused, or are sharing, his pleasure conclude—naturally enough—that he is "intelligent."

When he is displeased he is slow, stubborn, and those who have provoked his displeasure, or who disagree with him, conclude—equally naturally—that he is "stupid."

But this, to me, does not mean that he is not an intelligent person; it means that he is a person whose very excellent intellectual equipment would entitle him to be called intelligent, were it not for the fact that he refuses to be intelligent whenever his mind tells him something that runs counter to his emotional desires.

Again you may say that this is a subtle distinction; and again I would reply that to my mind it is an important one.

Finally, the same reasoning applies to Mr. Roosevelt's alleged superficiality. I am perfectly certain that his mind is capable of delving deeply into a subject. I have seen him delve into subjects in which he was interested. Ask him something about ships and see if you find him "superficial." Or ask him something about party politics.

On the other hand, he is undeniably and shockingly superficial about anything that relates to economics and particularly about anything that relates to finance. This is not, I think, because he is incapable of grasping these subjects, but because he does not like them and therefore refuses to make any great effort to understand them.

Nor is all this, to my way of thinking, anything very extraordinary. We are all like that in greater or less degree. The extraordinary part about Mr. Roosevelt is the extent to which the whole pattern of his living and thinking is woven around his emotional desires, predilections, and prejudices.

Mr. Roosevelt gives me the impression that he can really believe what he wants to believe, really think what he wants to think, and really remember what he wants to remember, to a greater extent than anyone I have ever known.

It is always dangerous to attempt to interpret the emotional motivation in another human being; it is difficult enough to interpret one's own. Nevertheless, since Mr. Roosevelt is so largely governed by his emotions, it becomes highly important to try to understand as much as possible what sort of emotional drive supplies the motive power behind his actions.

Knowing that I am here indulging not only in hypothesis but in a perfectly obvious oversimplification, I should say that Mr. Roosevelt is motivated primarily by two desires: the desire "to do good," and the desire "to be liked and admired."

In Mr. Roosevelt there is, I think, a real humanitarian desire to make life more pleasant, or at least more bearable, to the greatest possible number of people. In Mr. Roosevelt there is likewise, if I am not mistaken, an intellectual realization that neither he nor any other human being can do very much in this direction. The conflict of the desire which would like to do much, and the intellectual realization that there is but little that can be done, results, in Mr. Roosevelt, in a feverish assertion of the desire in the shape of an unfulfillable promise.

And the more his mind tells him that he is promising the impossible, the more vehemently Mr. Roosevelt is driven by his desire to reaffirm and amplify the promise.

It is this inner conflict which, as I see it, makes a travesty of Mr. Roosevelt's attempts at leadership, and which renders him incapable of following any consistent course—except the course of seeking the maximum of popular approval.

The leader of a democracy such as ours must, to be sure, carry out the will of the people; but he cannot do this by trying to please all of the people all of the time any more than he can "fool all of the people all of the time." Mr. Roosevelt's desire to be liked and admired has led him—and will, I fear, continue to lead him—to try to please all of the people all of the time by compromising where oftentimes he should dig in and fight.

Mr. Roosevelt, because he wants to be pleasant and agreeable to everyone, does not realize that there are some things on which no compromise is possible.

The sanctity of a promise, for example, can only be preserved intact or destroyed.

One is either a person whose word can be relied on—or one is not.

Before stating my conclusion in answer to our fourth and last question, there is one other point which seems to me worth touching upon.

You will remember Mr. Lippmann said of the President that "his mind is not very clear, his purposes are not simple, and his methods are not direct."

We have discussed the reasons why his mind is "not very clear"; we have seen why his "purposes are not simple"—because both his mind and his purposes are dominated by his necessarily ever shifting concept of what will make him popular and what will make him feel that he is "doing good."

But we have not yet considered why his "methods are not direct."

I am not sure that I know. I think it is partly because of the absence of any clear goal or plan, but also I think it is more than that: I think Mr. Roosevelt has a definite liking for the devious as opposed to the direct, for the complicated as opposed to the simple, and for the masked flank attack as opposed to the direct frontal assault.

He has this liking, I think, because it makes him feel superior to make everyone think he is going to do one thing, and then do another. That is being "smart" or "clever."

To feint at the center and then launch an attack upon the enemy's unsuspecting flank is of course what every good general will do. It is good tactics.

The trouble is that Mr. Roosevelt—as I see it —is not a good general. He is an excellent tactician; he can and does frequently conceal his real movement under a most convincing sham attack; but the trouble is that he conceals it, not only from the enemy, but from his own corps commanders and general staff. Sometimes, I think, he even conceals it from himself.

An excellent example of this was furnished by Mr. Roosevelt's hectic maneuvers in regard to the recent tax proposals, which left no one more hopelessly confused than Senators Harrison and Robinson, his own leaders in the Senate, whose actions he repudiated.

All this is simply saying in another way what I have said before. Since Mr. Roosevelt as a general has no definite plan of campaign and no definite objective—except the desire to be acclaimed a great general—he tends to lead his troops in a series of brilliant tactical maneuvers, which would certainly often "outwit" the enemy, if there were a definite enemy, and which would enable him probably to gain his objective—if he had an objective.

Thus it seems to me that "the desire to be clever" is a fault in Mr. Roosevelt, whereas, in a man less dominated by the passive desire for popularity and more activated by a definite striving toward an objective goal, it might be a great asset.

I am afraid that it is "the desire to be clever" that has led Mr. Roosevelt into some of his worst errors.

He thought he was being "clever" when he tried to satisfy the inflationists by letting them pass the "permissive" Thomas Amendment to the original Agricultural Act, rather than taking a firm stand against greenbacks.

He thought he was being "clever" when he made the first of his many compromises with the so-called "Silver Bloc."

He thought he was being "clever" when he tried to steal Huey Long's thunder by suddenly coming out with his "soak the rich" tax message.

None of these, and countless similar actions, were really "clever" or "smart," because they were all ineffective in satisfying the "radical" groups or individuals whom they were supposed to satisfy, and, on the other hand, definitely led Mr. Roosevelt to go much further in the various directions desired by the "radicals" than he originally had any idea or intention of going.

And so my answer to our fourth and last question is this:

I think Mr. Roosevelt's nature is such as to make him, in the sense of party politics, an ideal popular candidate for office, but an ineffective and dangerous incumbent, once he is elected.

And further, I think that those qualities of showmanship rather than statesmanship, which Mr. Roosevelt possesses and which may have been useful in the winter of 1932–1933, are certainly not the qualities which will be needed in the White House from here on.

# 5

## CONCLUSION

AT THE BEGINNING of this book I defined the basis of appraisal upon which I was going to try to tell you as simply and as convincingly as possible why I for one do not think Mr. Roosevelt should be reëlected President of the United States.

In the preceding chapters I have set forth my reasons for thinking:

1. That Mr. Roosevelt, as President, carried out a few of the less important promises he made when a candidate for that office; that he failed to carry out a far greater number of the more important; and that he fulfilled in very large measure the promises that had been made by the Socialist candidate Mr. Norman Thomas.

2. That Mr. Roosevelt's present purpose is to give the nation a "more abundant life" by first vesting in a central federal bureaucracy headed by himself complete dictatorial powers over all the factors that affect the economic and social life

of the nation, and, second, using these powers to produce, by executive management, the "more abundant life."

That this is a purpose to which we cannot subscribe, because:

a) To accomplish this purpose means to substitute for the American form of government a central "authoritarian" state, along the lines of the various European experiments in Socialism and dictatorship, and because,

b) The hope that, by thus sacrificing our traditional freedom, we shall attain a "more abundant life," is a vain and foolish hope, as no one has more cogently pointed out than Mr. Roosevelt himself, at the time when he was Governor of New York.

3. That Mr. Roosevelt's actions taken to accomplish his avowed purposes have been largely ineffective; and that, where they have been temporarily effective, their temporary usefulness has been outweighed by their disproportionate cost.

4. That Mr. Roosevelt's individuality is such as to make him an ineffective and dangerous man to have in the White House, because his actions and intellectual processes are too greatly dominated by his emotions, and because his emotional drive is primarily an inordinate desire for popularity.

That is my story. Those are my convictions. The reader must take them, modify them, or leave them, to suit her or himself.

If you agree with me in whole or in large measure, you may or may not agree with my conclusion that, barring an extreme radical or an extreme reactionary, almost any citizen of integrity would be better to have in the White House than Mr. Roosevelt.

But, whether you agree or not, this much, I think, is clear:

Mr. Roosevelt has definitely determined the issue on which he must go to the country next year. He has definitely determined that the issue shall be whether or not we want to abandon the home rule principle, states' rights, and the fundamental concept of our Constitutional democracy in order to make a try for the "more abundant life" by setting up a bureaucratic dictatorship of "master minds" in Washington.

He has definitely asked us to decide whether we agree with Governor Roosevelt, who in 1930 condemned such an attempt, or with President Roosevelt, who in 1935 recommends it.

Whether or not Mr. Roosevelt admits this to be the issue matters not in the least. His actions and his recent utterances can leave not the slightest room for doubt.

Bear in mind that highly significant speech about the farmer "being a lord on his own farm."

Bear in mind the "horse-and-buggy" attack upon the NRA decision.

Bear in mind the unconstitutional removal without cause of Commissioner Humphrey from the Federal Trade Commission, because, "You will, I know, realize that your mind and my mind do not go along together on either the policies or the administering of the Federal Trade Commission, and, frankly, I think it is best for the people of this country that I should have a full confidence." (The Supreme Court unanimously declared this removal of Commissioner Humphrey unconstitutional.)

Bear in mind the administration-sponsored bill to withdraw from citizens the right to obtain through the courts whatever damages they may suffer through the devaluation of the dollar.

Bear in mind the administration-sponsored effort to have Congress pass a law making it impossible for citizens to recover moneys paid under a tax, in the event that such tax should later be held unconstitutional.

And don't ever forget that remarkably frank letter to Chairman Hill, in which the President expressed the hope that Congress would not let "any doubts as to the constitutionality, however reasonable," stand in the way of the proposed legislation.

If Mr. Roosevelt says that this is not the issue, that he is only trying to save the American order from itself, that reëlecting him is the only way to prevent revolution, and so forth and so on, I for one shall only smile.

Not because I shall not think he believes what he is saying.

Not because I shall doubt his much discussed "sincerity."

But because I know that Mr. Roosevelt can make himself believe what he wants to believe, think what he wants to think, and remember what he wants to remember.

Because I know that in talking to a conservative he wants—really wants—to be a conservative; and that in talking to a radical he wants to show him that he knows more about redistributing wealth than the late Senator Long.

Because I know, in other words, that there is only one real driving force in Mr. Roosevelt, and that is the desire to be liked and admired by the greatest possible number of people.

That is why I have given this book the somewhat flippant title:

"HELL BENT FOR ELECTION."